FULL SIGHT OF HER

Patrick Wright's moving, powerful *Full Sight of Her* takes its reader to fearful, anxious places, describing love and care which come under terrible pressure. Wright's bereaved, often bereft poems find words to protect the self, this lover who must become a 'widower, prizing thumbnails' in the book's densely visual poems, a man for whom even the 'town scenery is full of tears'. Throughout, Wright finds forms which offer some protection for the bare feelings and memories the poems navigate, stanzas and shapes which mean that, as he writes, 'I proceed on the basis of metaphor' even as he knows that he must 'wear the scar.'
– JOHN McAULIFFE

Patrick Wright has developed distinctive poetic approaches to emotion in these poems which are by turns arresting and moving. 'I'm here as witness' a speaker says and it is as if that protagonist could be all of us, though also singularly themselves. Despite the loss and the grief, this book conveys a powerful sense of shared humanity. Linguistically and syntactically challenging at times, the pay-off for a reader is a unity of purpose which pervades the collection. Pressured lines give way to striking images and recurring motifs. The poem itself, its ability to hear 'sea sounds/ of the motorway' is a place where an almost forensic sifting takes place, ensuring poems which demand and reward an equal and acute attention.
– SIOBHAN CAMPBELL

This powerfully moving, even harrowing, collection cuts to the very heart of loss. Yet it also celebrates a very special, strong, sensuous love that over-rides mental illness, an age-gap, and eventual physical illness, leading to the slow death of the beloved. These poems, while honouring his lover for her talent as an artist, her femininity and eccentricity, do not shy away from the graphic. They explore, analyse and sensitively articulate, through startling vivid images, often impressionistic and surreal, a whole world of time present and past, urban landscapes, seasides, claustrophobic interiors, ghosts, different kinds of sight and the liminal, questionable borders between dream and reality in a recognisable world of medicines, mobile phones and selfies. The haunting final elegy unites all the previous poems and demonstrates achingly 'the price of love'. This is a poet to watch.
– PATRICIA MCCARTHY

Patrick Wright

Full Sight Of Her

First published in 2020
by The Black Spring Press Group
Suite 333, 19-21 Crawford Street
Marylebone, London W1H 1PJ
United Kingdom

Cover design and typeset by Edwin Smet

The right of Patrick Wright to be identified as the author,
and Kim Parkinson to be identified as the artist of this work has
been asserted in accordance with section 77 of the Copyright,
Designs and Patents Act 1988

ISBN 978-1-913606-04-6

WWW.EYEWEARPUBLISHING.COM

In Memory of Kim

Patrick Wright
was born in Manchester's edgelands in 1979.
He has been shortlisted for the Bridport Prize, and his poems
have appeared in several magazines, most recently *Agenda*, *The
High Window*, and *Wasafiri*. He has been twice included in
The Best New British and Irish Poets anthology.
He teaches English Literature and Creative Writing at
the Open University and lives in Manchester.

TABLE OF CONTENTS

Were it not for shadows,
there would be no beauty

Jun'ichirō Tanizaki

THE DECLINE OF DAYDREAMING

Once propped against the brickwork,
head wedged by a drainpipe, I dreamt
behind it – the back of junior school
with ghosts of bins, a butterfly garden,
rainbows thrown on a skirting board.
Estranged by the clamour of boys'
bravado – games of tag, toy fights,
Batman cards – the mask of actors
slipped to stick-men chalked on walls.
How perverse, enticed by shadows on
hopscotch gravel, to sneak by dinner-
ladies, cooling vents, listen for voices.
Such hideouts would concern a host
of doctors. Much I had in the seconds
before a scolding, the drag to the yard.
I seek this windbreak, *The Soothsayer's
Recompense*; arcades, colonnades, sweet
Ariadne; the lull of masts, flags, fixed
steam of a train. Why is that vacuum
words blew into now full of iPhones,
apps blocking signals? – *der Stimmung*,
green skies, queasy light. Where I begin
has always been Turin. A space for all
questions to confound, with the break
which led me to leave the playground.

AUBADE

The sun gives the curtain the look of love,
its light through a bride's organza,
as I leave your rapid eyes and wonder
how far you've gone with the tramadol.
Somewhere you're lucid, scaring yourself
I'll leave you.

    The meds prolong the limen between
what's real and not, as I rehearse words
to reassure. We are only six hours
from the rush of oxytocin, from a feeling
everything's okay. Yet where you are
is dysphoric again.

    I can tell from the way you blink
out of your paradoxical sleep
and then come a litany of nightmares.
They sound like times I've overdosed
on valerian – less so a narrative
than a kaleidoscope of selves.

    I kiss you through your fringe,
say all is sweet, repeat, know this
and a tisane should do the trick.
Yet our thoughts collect from separate
pillows, where we ring-fence the fear,
as we turn each night and jilt each other.

THE UNWAKING

How I hate to have to wake you
Sunday morning   like the man from Porlock.
Inside your dream   unspooling
feels the most sacred thing
even if spring is full of itself   near noon.
I can't hold off from rousing you
giddy with our day ahead
the multitude of memories we could make.
Again that pang as you describe the cut
end of a tape   a story left unfinished
and never know now   ever again
where the truncated scene might have led.

So I step back to my notepad and pen
let your head fall back
to the sheet   redeem something at least
of my voice stealing from the soundless air
the far deeper intimacy of you
alone in a bedroom without me.
Just words on a page offer
some flawed equivalence   having broken off
from stroking your hand   saying your name
how our day will prove better
than where you've been   and return to again.

BEFORE IT ALL STARTS UP

Outside from the Scarisbrick third floor window
a brass band takes a break down a ginnel.
There they clump, cups in hands. Now, as we
fold up our slacks, still half-inside our dreams,
I see the band salute, limbs of automata.
She can't be sure it's real, the line between

sleep and day more like a hinterland.
And now's such a time, where, before the maid
arrives, distracted from her rucksack,
she's enthralled by the show of light
splayed on walls through diamanté crystal.
I love how she dovetails one to the other,

how that dance of sunlight and soldiers is
choreographed. Such is the meaning she gives
to the morning, as I fall in love, again,
her mind gone 'quantum' (manic?), beyond
the band and businesses opening outside.
She makes sense of how it all knits together

as she lets a floral print frock fall down
her thighs, sprays lavender on the bit below
her collarbone. My eyes go to her fibula
or *fetlocks* as she calls them, as she passes me
the sun block, jushes my neck gaiter with forgotten
scent, my torso with protective witch hazel.
As usual we share her Clarins rose. Then she wonders
if the bouclé coat might go better, the weather as it is.

Here is happiness as the world filters in,
as the fan whirs on, in moments of just us
at the origin of things, before the drums
and horn start up again, before we're set to leave,
as she fashions a bandana out of lingerie,
when, forewarned by light, she wears a final skin.

THE BALCONY ON BARKER SUITE

Below are balconies, abandoned sun loungers,
dreams of heads full of flowers.
All is serene through the balustrades.
My window shows off chevrons,
a zebra crossing – humbug, magpie? –

hessian either side of anti-pigeon spikes.
Four-poster, scarves to tie her up with,
in the Rufford Room ebony tower
of faux Renoir silkscreens, TV to Al Jazeera.
On the carpet her nude feet are shy.

Outside, machines are slowing, slowly.
East Bank tapers inland, where rain blitzkriegs
heavy goods vehicles, heading to Hull.
A hundred miles of *To-let* signs,
To-let signs saying the economy's on the slide.

Clouds gather like shorn wool.
I'm done listening about the Syrians,
refugees this evening, while she talks
of tomorrow, the *maître d'*, pedicure, lotion, spa,
undresses in slow increments.

The fountain flows even though it's September.
Buses hiss on their suspensions.
The road's a vein some distance from the heart.
Earlier a Merc and a wedding gown;
now revellers, rat-arsed scousers

under a mezzanine sky. Carbon monoxide,
motorbikes – Kawasakis? – rev and fly.
Fire engines ride to some out of sight dry riser.
Sirens cut the mood like power tools.
She asks: 'Are we gargoyles or angels?'

A sunset? No sunset in sight: upstairs
rooms, bulbless, unused, windows blood-
orange, then gold. The sky's a sheet
of tarpaulin and cigarette smoulder.
When it ends, it ends as an aquarium.

Each light ticks on with a separate timer:
lamps droop – fuchsias? – clock of the clock
tower, spacecraft beacons, taxis off tarmac…
Chimneys erect like observatories,
as stars hang patiently the other side.

BEACHCOMBERS

We slalom through dunes and dead Christmas trees,
down to a harbour of litter shingle treasure:
fibreglass bits of boats, flung soles, sea-weathered oak,
salvaged from beds of stone and mica.

Our prize find, a doll's severed head, its hair spiked
with sand. Otherwise, the birch-wood she asks for:
sticks carved into limbs 'for Barbie and Ken amputees'.

(Her home, indeed, a hospital of foundlings,
unfortunates, awaiting her bag and a reason to be.)

She roams for hours, conceiving of some assemblage;
her cane brushing boulders of tobacco,
tossing back as trash things that 'need more sea',
such as a frisbee of tooth-marks, left tainted.

Now a birch branch described, burnt by a campfire,
its end bent like a boomerang.

She says straightaway: 'it's a fat finger, we cannot leave
till the fingers and thumb are found from what clearly *is*
a giant hand!'. Her grin, gothic, she turns it round,
sure it's a ballerina on her toes. When home she'll paint

false nails over the stump, fit a shoe over the foot.
I suggest a fishnet pull-up, a pirate's peg leg or club.
I hold another branch next to it, make a harp.

We laugh, squeeze each other. A kite ripples like a tiny
diamond. She kisses me on the cheek for not knowing
the 'pointy thing' is Blackpool Tower.

ANTICS

I love your tumbleweed moments
giving eyes the glaze
in shops when you offer a thought
on urban etiquette;
let out your dream of dinosaurs
and hear it fall
into the mundane;
or use words like *finials*
as the youngsters check their phones.

I love how you're out of sync
when they look to me
as you show off your knitted trolley,
your decoupaged case;
how you're fine on fifty milligrams
when the world panics
has you shut away
all because of your antics
when you talk to the wind or stream.

I love how you want to make a box
lined with batik, fill it with odds,
brought up on *Bagpuss* and *The Wombles*;
your flash performance
in vocal-centric style;
how you rick a home-made chimney
out of Slimfast tins;
how you turn an Ikea nightmare into
something Japanese.

17

IT STARTS WITH HER AWKWARD HAIRLINE

the bit behind her ear, along the bone,
I accidentally on purpose stroke
as the comb starts to move freely. Her head
between my knees, a kiss on her lobe –
something she wouldn't get in a salon –
and fingers that look for further lugs.
The part along her neck too, the transition
of neck and scalp, like beach and sea
where hairs grow upward. Once she
hid it from view, calling herself simian;
and now it's a *zone*, one she says I made
for her, that wasn't there before.
I kiss this too, following the teeth
and say: 'Repeat: "I am beautiful."'
She says: '*You* are beautiful.' Still that's
better than it was, as I work on her
one stage at a time. All that's left now
is the style, and I start back with the comb,
fan out a fringe as she watches TV.
The filaments are the days we've got left.
Roots of silver I cover with cosmic blue.
And here an echo, almost unheard.
I did this for another. I was smaller.
We had an electric fire. She wore
rollers. And it was far from a chore,
rather utmost pleasure, untangling
strands until they flowed like rivers.
I still seem to know how much pressure
to apply, not to hurt a single nerve.

ANGEL OF THE COSMOS (THE MURAL)

As you stretch on a chair and wear something throw-on, the mural
   you make is streaked in ultramarine; globes of peeled paper, plaster;
forms you infer from light – alien super earths
   all brought together in the galactic centre.

I observe and confer from the cherry red swivel chair
   your itch to smash the kentia palm vase, stick slivers as mirrors,
get someone else to curse themselves and shape its smithereens,
   encrust those seas with shrapnel. Your *what-ifs* cascade –

like muji frames, tiled across and over; dabbing toenail varnish,
   red to accentuate the pareidolic skull; crackle glazing
the skirting boards – Nitromors, tangerine dream, fireburst
   with shocks of magenta; stick lights lighting the unsunned corner.

You burn magnesium-bright as I come over occasionally, brush
   your feet through your chaussettes, Vangelis playing in the background,
as you sublimate with a scourer and matt glissando strokes.
   I trust your guesstimations when you say this is destined to be

a true aurora borealis of coloured auras and orbs.
   You unpeel again accretions of layers, a neighbour's *décor* –
greens, dirty mushrooms – and insist on a star field over it,
   starboard side; plumes of hot gas in a nebula. You stand back,

hands on hips, head cocked to one side, rhapsodised, zoned
   somewhere remote, full flow. I have to temper though the madcap
proposals, since you would happily bolt a chair
   up there or fibre-optic cable, fix false limbs and eyelashes

on paint, when I would go for the more sensible gold leaf.
   And when not looking you write *avec le fântome* in lipstick
on the shabby chic shelves – shocking pink, freshly sponged boho,
   old rose – too manic to include me or kiss.

INTERMISSIONS

Through the early hours of the horror channel,
what you take perhaps is a soundtrack
or webwork of narrative,
as you strain close to the plasma screen like a Cyclops,
infer from the strobing scenes
what the denouement might mean.
Films, always unfinished,
or you're left afterwards with only dialogue or melodic leaps.
How easily it slips into waking dreams,
as you splice your own dailies,
stitch together the outtakes,
enjoy the hallucinations.
Through your impairment, it's the lacunae you embrace,
writing your own scripts, as I push, next day, for some sort of précis.

What unspools are two movies fused together
or it seems like your own edit.
And, since projected, you text me interpretations,
or sometimes you predict the ending.
It's so uncanny, just before the sky turns blue,
as you fugue on your sofa,
aerial lead intermittent, between stations, time zones,
allowing a Hitchcock to bleed seamlessly
into news reports of psychopaths,
how the clatter in the kitchen *is* a poltergeist,
the urban hum a spacecraft hovering over your social housing.

What for me might be street frolics is, for you,
a banshee without question,
especially this hour, this distance,
more than a postcode between us,
where I offer no audio description.
I have to leave you to your clicker,
so you might hear amid the white noise,
messages, as sleep comes and rolls the credits.

THE BLIND PHOTOGRAPHER

How is it you see through your pinhole?
What you call a two o'clock aperture lets in
shocks of pink, giving-it-large green, magenta;
the rest bleach. Form for you is like gazing
through frosted glass so that lamps look like
daubs of hue or big fish scales. Sometimes
you catch shadows on ceilings. Once, back-lit
against encroaching sea, when the light
was perfect, my black fleece gifted us
contrast: you saw a jelly bean.

You defy prejudice. Since the days
of knowing your right eye would never work
and your left would slowly deteriorate,
you set about learning the golden mean,
Quattrocento, single point, to conceive
what it might be like for things to fall
outwards. You've never known three
dimensions, but spent a lifetime projecting
arcades. In managing this, you're a seer.
Your eye *is* a camera; and with knowledge

of how things lit before it all started
to fade, readying yourself in advance, by
looking for forty years at the world twice
as hard as twenty-twenties among us,
you're an artist. Your Flickr page reads
as a diary of long goodbyes, a path to
abstraction – light documents you call them;
more like *visions*, the closest analogue
to your periphery, how you share a lens
through the graininess of pixel devices.

You tell me the blind world is beautiful,
that once it's possible to get past the fear
everything becomes cosseted, inward.
Your genius hangs everywhere. I love
what you do with sunlight, how you're able
to capture the limits through small spirit
lights that fall on walls without most of us
noticing. I love how you call them *numens*,
invoking all that's lost in the world
as blocks of visitation on contact paper.

DOUBLE BLIND

Unsighted, eyes on the pillow next to mine;
a chance alignment where, for a moment,
your gaze holds mine – or what I *guess* has happened.
And if that happened would it consummate our touch,
our breath, our everything else?

Sometimes you talk as if you died already
and this guise is merely a ghost, and that's
what love aligns with –
                                   or am I smitten
by the sighted you from ten years ago,
thus a different you, different us or incarnation?
            Rather it's the age gap that dilates
year by year. Even close up, this almost
nose-to-nose conjures an image of me
at twenty-four – lips unkissed in a cafe –

as I stay fixed. On your side no elixir works,
nothing to reassure against a thought all this
is temporary, *we* are temporary, a rose tint
over pity, or just a phase I'm passing through.

HIGHTOWN

More distant, our shadows stretch
apart: closer now to the MOD
warning sign, I read *rifle range, keep out*.
When the beacon light's red
shells mean something else:

Stop here. Listen.
Keep look for that foreshore ghost
stuck like a thin-man sentinel.

Offshore turbines twirl
like toy windmills, as I upset
the heads of flounders, flies,
terns yarring the word
trespasser.

Then the expanse:
sounds, like airstrip silence
slinking through slack and sand-hills.

As I glance back, you're still,
statuesque, black against the Alt's
edge and estuary, fixed as the gas rig
funnelling its lone star;

conscious of rounds
which ricochet the headland,
of crosshairs trained on veins.

Your mind struggles
to reconcile the sand lizards

and shrapnel, the scent of asparagus
beds with cadets or hum
of a razor wire fence;

whereas I lament
the lack of a lifeguard
and each step it took
to find ourselves.

THE MANIA DOLL ON SOUTHPORT PIER

In the days of the roller skating rink
we had one called Pepe. Boxed-in,
his pierrot wrists jangled, his feet
impaled with strings. Now this

as you tilt your head like him,
your hat of paper cloche, ridiculous;
deadpan behind a blind woman's shades,
strange as a geisha.

He laughs and laughs as if his head
might fall off. And the more he laughs
the more you regress to the time
you said they thought you sick

for not being entertained. Young
as I was in the roller skating rink,
you recalled how you slunk among kids
your age, and went catatonic

as your peers laughed and laughed
at the freak show, by the bendy mirrors
and holograms, the clownish hordes.
You went serious and shy

as you do so now: shoulders stiff, a form,
letting your bag of chips go cold.
The kiosk shadows, they crane.
A coin-operated doll ends the show.

OUT OF SEASON

We didn't look at the sky once
as jets drowned out our lips on the precinct.

We talked of upcycling bookshelves
out of larch-lap fruit crates;
how to haiku the sun through toy windmills.

Of all days we had to visit, an airshow!
It spoiled our love for the derelict.

We fretted over candy sticks, gelaterias,
dodderers, strollers, queues for candy-floss.

With hotels booked up, the crowd to be lost,
we nudged past machismo-camouflage,

lads with dads (what chance do *they* have?) –
to a sublime expanse, towards the esplanade.

We didn't look at the sky once.

We held hands, circled a closed-down
amusement park, fenced-off,
rides stopped, arcade machines unplugged.

We, in recession-hit Southport,
agreed how we preferred the ghost train shut

for carousel horses to stay in shadow

dodgems to remain passengerless

the crazy golf course to blow its paper cups.

AUTOMAT

BLACK MIRROR

Coming back to your face prone in a drink,
void of its mirror, like the one in *Chop Suey*
– skin painted, look of downcast America.
Such a dead-ringer for the woman I met –
her bell hat pulled tight, shyly
uninviting conversation. Her gaze
echoing espresso, sleeves indifferent to sex.

I keep coming back to this face,
these legs, the brightest bit. The loneliness
I cannot fathom. She sits leaden, opposite
me in a deli, eyes inward, like I never was.

Your face, coming back to it, crops up
in facsimiles: Lowry's *Portrait of Ann* –
a brunette, a type, some elusive X –
or the paleness, cheekbones, lips?

I can't escape this same face;
and each time, each beloved
gets overlaid with the image,
as we arrange to rendezvous,
sometimes miss each other,
leave a text, then disconnect.

BLACK MIRROR

How changed since the *tain* was a bedroom portal –
a tilted dimension just as real, a land to be lived in –
the mind enclosed in my boyhood photo, far wall.

Now a mirror, dark as the life I made for myself,
a gift bought on day-release from a psycho ward –
fears of geopathic stress, parabens, bad feng shui –
which sits here studded with a Swarovski tree.

Of all things why this? The absurdity of opulence,
a square of licorice; something that will cheer us
like mums buy sweets after accidents. Gone awol,

gazing in sync, faces, *folie à deux*, fused under sun;
androgyne, unsure who sported the stolen peejays
out a cell we escaped, of nurse patrols, intercoms...

Same in the lounge plasma screen or the window
starting to turn pitch and inward – phantoms all –
the sky now dimmed: as Chinese lanterns morph

to a lampshade, I ask what's there behind the eye,
whether it's me or if in fact we merge and it's *her*
through such vertical lakes, shades of noir, inside
the bezels of all glass surfaces around the flat.

SELFIES

No one takes a photo at a funeral.
Forgetting is all that's real.
Whereas, for you, each pic's a reminder
that part of you is dead.
You pose as if sight lives,
like you've painted, each time,
false eyes over eyelids,
and still know, precisely, how light
prints, done selflessly, for my benefit.

Each time, *click*, an archivist,
filing j-pegs on folders of my Seagate.
One-sided: you have no say
in the lighting, no sense of which angle,
I think, shows off your
better side. Take this one:
finger-flashing your engagement ring,
us doing that cheek-to-cheek thing.

Custodian of this solo gallery,
have I robbed your life review,
pried into a preview of unseen
arms-entangled images, of us,
lived perhaps twofold or more
intensely? Beyond each selfie
embellished at the back of your
brain (the darkroom of your mind)
there's *me*: each evening bereaved,
a widower, prizing thumbnails,
dense with everything. As I describe
to you my smile, your blindness
rehearses the grief we've denied.

ANOTHER KIND OF HOUSE

From scratch, a house built from the ruins up
follows no architectural plan, save for what's
dreamt over several times. No-one I say in their
right mind would climb *that* staircase, unsure
steps, less than a match for what's safe, abstract.

At the shop, I grab only greys and whites,
sometimes greens for the lichened parts.
As cement, the studs go fine; though the
shapes are make-do, unhewn for the task.

It's devised as a homage to Lovecraft, rooms
within rooms, alcoves, and a walled-up cat.
I've hinged it like a dolls' house, so its doors
can be swung open to sunlight, or lamp light
might trail through the table legs, a strange star.

Residents thus far comprise of a mermaid,
a gingerbread man, a cliché ghoul in Day-Glo
sheets. I proceed on the basis of metaphor.
Or is this my actual house?, come to think.

SOME DEFORMED FUKUSHIMA DAISIES

It's gone viral
from the outskirts of the Fukushima nuclear plant.
Close-ups with the highest res' of megapixels.
Heads fused as conjoined twins
cresting at the lips or stigmas.
Any other context and they'd be said to be kissing,
though it would have to be eternal.
And how might they eat?
Their enclosed faces spurn the sun
whose fusion is a saviour.
It beats down regardless.
And their stems are bent over double
like spines of grown-old-together brothers.

Shasta daisies born of a tsunami
show off their skins of leukaemia bruises,
thyroid cysts,
like pubescent nightmares of another Windscale,
another Chernobyl.
And as I google the meaning of *meltdown*
I stumble over stories of evacuees,
articles on damage done to genes,
what the mutant reality is
of kids whose heritage begins
in rhizomes, grasses, trees,
toxic hospital units.

No matter what the cause is,
whether malformed stalks are metaphors,
they can't stop us from our sleepwalk.
And this is the way the planet talks,

like the body talks with its symptoms
or the mind talks with neuroses –
if only we'd *listen*
and re-learn how to read signs and ciphers
rather than rely on pills – consider hysteria,
no longer think of sadness as an illness
or think of madness as a lesion.
Perhaps the heart truly has its reasons,
and *we* are the daisies,
we are the fallout,
the Twitter feeds our babies.

ELISIONS

Facing you in the loggia, as you hand-comb
your sputnik-shaped bed hair –
the tuft especially you say is my fault –
I guess this is intimacy. On the surface
husband and wife, minutiae and erogenous zones
all known, the familiar eyes I wake to,
half-moon and dopily assured, the morning
ritual of Earl Grey and powdered milk,
your query about the sun, sieved
through voile curtains, or some dark
surreal you dragged out of your dream.

    Is it for me to discern where the day-
light begins? Certain words go unsaid
in the dictionary, ones I've bracketed
as they remind us of the *other woman*,
of London, clonazepam; the episodes
we hope are behind us. Have I silenced
that part of you – of phantasms, threats,
fugues, of analysing words like *concubine*
over and over? Or does it stay remote?

    This is for your sake: not saying words like *fox*
(that's her surname), once chained to *Fuchs*,
then *fucks*, as you felt those words betrayed
my *philandering side*. And now no signs
as we breakfast before another act. To check
each word, not trigger you, reflect on it fast,
think at all times of your otherness – the *-osis*.
I was faithful all along.

THE GHOST ROOM

All day she's been at the craft table punching butterflies
out of stolen *Vogue* issues. She's making me a sconce
to say sorry – sorry for the abuse blamed on the moon –
one panel of flatpack upped with usual flair into
something stellar; and on those shelves, ricked with gravity –
'jenga' – she's arranged for us a mirror.

Her chandelier stuns like a jellyfish, wedding dress
gauze wrapped improv round the fitting. It sways a little.
Then the mannequin propped by her balcony, 'Ernest'.
We talk of him as if he's our son (since we understand
by now we aren't going to have one), and our daughter's
the Bratz doll who basks in a fairy castle.

Nowhere is anything sane – and this is us, the room
built on schisms. We're in a world of white-themed-things,
apparitions; not quite meeting. And beneath the frolics
I can't help wonder why her children don't make contact.
Yes, this is us, where handbags amass like surrogate wombs;
where the joke begins to wear itself thin.

SERTRALINE

These empty blister packs left around the flat
are prerequisites.   This is the price of love,
or what this is.   And the side effects –
the longer sleep, the occasional bleed... –
are signs things are working.   We are working:
I can't remember the last time the crisis team
were called.   When the allegations came,
I forgave you like a Christian.

NULLABY

The only sounds this evening are the solitary
pulse of an electric aromatic diffuser
and occasional sea-echo from the fridge.
The diffuser purrs in the hearth corner
I need to brighten by clearing out her
batik scarves – black-starred with mold –
driftwood planks for doll prosthetics
and a hundred keepsake carrier bags.
    The motor fans out a nimbus of steam
lit by a revolving door of gels – blues,
pinks, cerise. Her concoction still somehow
knocks me out. Christmas oil, lavender, tea tree.
    Higher towards the ceiling throbs
an infrared lamp – a binary companion? –
not some common-or-garden sixty watt thing
but a heat-emitting glowworm
she nursed my sacroiliac with. It casts the room
as a boudoir, a private red light district.

Outside the security bulb clicks on for a minute.
Squinting out the window
a refuse sack of shoes. Naked back to bed,
the pillow's indent, a single hair, a scattering
of hearts *punkt* out of what I called junk;
for her something to upcycle...
    And the down-cycling of us, trashing
our trust, finding the sinister in a snowflake –
a borderline state? an inner script?
Is she in London with the lunatics?
Is she in the care of the services?
Couldn't stand her gaslighting the flat.

No arguing over exclusive. No texts firing
gatling gun. No love by a thousand cuts.
Headfucked till I switched her off. And still
the psychic stabs: *you have destroyed me*...
Her hour of need, I refused a key, let her
sleep on benches, walk out into traffic.

No clock ticks – an iPod charges
with the alarm set for eight on chimes.
Those grate the least. For now
the milk float roads are less lit than dreams –
dreams of finding her: an asylum visit
where no one speaks. I close my eyes,
come close to agreeing the gust really *is*
the ghost of a train, confuse words for things,
fear the slightest creak of wood contracting
when the boiler sleeps.
        A car slushes the latest downpour
and strobes its headlights down the wardrobe –
a friend for a second...
        And I'm at it again. How there's nothing
to find sane this red-eyed morning –
the upped dimmer-switch of dawn. How thoughts
find reflections in unwashed clothes on the carpet.
How the sun seems to rise without intent.

DOPPELGÄNGERS

The night is specious with streaks of neon
or ribbons of light in pavement pools.
They screen the sidereal, arc over the urban sky
as aircraft beacons on the high-rise scintillate
and dive, become like plasma of solar flares.

Things double: old-school double exposures.
Faces gurn to a Francis Bacon –
bourgeois masks oncoming from stations –
and glisten as rain hits their hoods,
alive like statues in cemetery dusk.
Here they come parading attaché cases:
all four-eyed with lunatic stares.

The glaze of car windows by the flyover
holds the day's dead-ringers, double-
takes, doppelgängers of the woman I miss.
Scenes not as they exist, more as if
her ghost unfolds layers, leans itself against
the gates of buildings, once stepped,
seared already in the most razed of spaces:

the cityscape, arterial roads, cobblestones,
tar and bitumen back streets,
wraiths and strays, vagabonds, towerblocks,
derelict mills, railway archways and quays;
a maze of ennui, Bruges with its belfries.

She dissipates in a stranger's wayward gait
or glance, the remainder in the ether
by a taxi rank or abandoned cinema,

a siren screaming through the district;
or frequents shadows of scaffolding,
temporary railings, leaving behind a trail
on the kerb of laughing gas canisters.

Buses blur towards me too-late numbers,
revellers spill out with sick, bloodstains,
slivers of glass, morph to zombies;
and I squint, too sober to see myself,
this freakshow in panelled hoardings.

FUGUE TO A SEASIDE TOWN

All the years gone wrong, in a blindfold
pin-in-the-map sort of place. No day trip or retreat,
more like a sun-drenched fire escape.

First an Italian ice cream parlour, let time
circle a while, peer down pipe-smoke boulevards,
let the seafronts blend into one another.

The lives un-lived, the doors that close;
the one seemingly I want is wedged open...
Out the window slide the zimmers;

soon I follow. A pilgrimage to metal birds
cast by a sky of clouds, adzed and surreal.
I long for their wings; my shoulder blades tickle.

Who knows what's left to bargain for
as I ghostwalk the Winter Garden, Assyrian Tower,
past faded pop glamour, then pause:

post-future teens, skateboards, the half-pipe,
BMX-ers, half-arsed nihilism, love letters scrawled
with aerosol. This once Sunset Coast,

I've dropped nothing, so why the psychedelia?
Like mosques once seen in place of factories
a seascape turns to a Lowry abstract;

a crisp packet promenade, spectral charabancs,
as shades placate on carborundum facades...
This must be, for some, *ataraxia* –

though the crisis comes for this alter ego,
at the nadir, when I swear mother's footprints
are somewhere near the Midland. Big decisions

rehearsed in the badlands, plain sight of Heysham,
thoughts of the nuclear. This, the unmarried
life. This is leisure and slow retirement.

DEPARTURES

'If I go quiet it's 'cos my phone just died.'
Outside, the station, a maniac on stilts:
something clattering, coming closer...
Behind me, a mannequin's fallen asleep,
earphones in, carriage quiet, totally still.
The other train, motionless, is one long
unending plantain, windows opaque.
Profiles of passengers, shadow puppets,
marionettes on strings, still where they sit.
My neck clicks as I scan, half panorama.
The sky's laughing and the driver's ill,
or dead, a screwdriver stabbed in his skull.
His engine's off and chewing gum
on the platform is too meaningful.
'I only have one percent on my battery left.'
Such moments come like a rehearsal.
My contacts list, sparse as the stars,
blinks under a colourless wash of cloud.
'For now I'll continue to type.' As the train
starts, the driver's miraculously survived,
a mechanoid now, made of metal. He
jolts the engine, builds momentum, moves
out, any direction. We move out, under
lozenge lamps, a fleeting face in the sky.
Houses pass: lines of teeth through
speeding glass, a plasma screen of back yards.
The foghorn startles like a coffin prised.
Now the scene slows, a station arrives;
the phone shuts down, turns to a slab...
Now the engine revs like a detonation.
The passenger wakes, tugs his earphones.
Now the mind becomes the animation.

HOMECOMING

Alighting the ninety-eight with a limp, I staggered
like an old man to the park I'd not been in
since I was five or thereabouts. There I was, weary.
A new generation of tiny feet on reins
occupied my space, as if I were a ghost.
Rain kept beading on the card I insisted on writing
and the trees were insufficient. Those words, so banal.
On a sheltered, terracotta wall, they missed the mark.

While dad was away in Beaumaris with *her*,
he welcomed me to a room of dust, financial concerns.
Kept awake by the low frequency hum, he'd less hair
than last time. I returned a pile of films, passed them
to his armchair, moulded to his skin. Slug trails
slavered the carpet. And to this he was blind.
Three cards made a makeshift shrine. A hard drive
entertained him. Mother – *God!* – would be devastated.

We talked about his online, Thai, she-male friend,
his neighbour sawing down his forty-foot
Aussie eucalyptus, the high school's new fence
that spoils his view from the hide;
Carl Sagan, metaphysics, whether dreams of the dead
are *more* than neurones firing unawares;
Liverpool transfers, government cuts, plantar fasciitis,
strategies of dealing with a conniving wife...

Outside, the window frame where she used to wash up
had the look of twelve years later.
Cotoneaster up the drainpipe left no aesthetic;
to us it was merely derelict. Together we trudged

across the diagonal path to find the absence
of Wi-Fi, the dolmen where the cat's now buried.
Didn't even notice the nettles sting.
Impressions lined up like clothes on a line.

Then back on the bus: town scenery full of tears,
too familiar, too used by time and advance.
I went so far into it, I began to blur the difference
between *this* and my bad dreams:
that perhaps the night really is the light, or vice versa.
How sick the stomach when those terrace houses slide by,
the terribly white Englishness in full May sunlight,
and the slow approach of the city, the choices we make in life.

ROLLER DISCO

Did I grow up in a circus?
Clearly a clown, coin-fed;
acrobats, sequins, a roller rink...
Clearly knife-throwers –
gangs aiming for my father's head.
He wore a disguise, an identikit.

Bulldozers grazing Odeon chairs,
ephemera of the flicks.
A recce of upstairs rooms –
guanoed sills, a Spider-Man figure,
Mad Max memorabilia,
a hint of perfumes, hairdos...

Unhomely. At the grand opening
I lost myself, far side of the rink
under a glitter-ball,
before skaters performed,
while mum mopped the entrance hall.
I'd go off on wheels –

a ghoul drawn to where, last night,
ribs broke on a barrier.
They told me tales –
a body walled up, unearthed in the work.
It wasn't in the news.
Or of a ghost or two.

Was it a haunted house?
The balcony's tasseled curtain:
the site of a tragic fall.

The silver of those strips, they'd twitch
on a breezeless upper floor –
the dark behind it. Then distracted:

after stories of cold spots,
chairs stacking up, unseen hands –
father busy with partners –
I moved to ankles, thighs, skirts
by a changing room door.
Was I the ghost? Was I always alone?

THE PROMONTORY AT BLACK POINT

Last night, snores filled the bunk, by Winnebagos
parked on rocks, while down the ladder the breaths
of mum swirled in prescient dark. Bagged up, helpless
on Hook Island, nothing else awake but the waves.

Lulling myself with vinyl waves, the bed took me
back to the bunk, the campsite, the familiar island –
same dens, coves, same cliffs, rocks, stones
skimmed before dark, the same call, same shadow of mum.

How in sleep can I say that's mum? Shipwrecks
jut their ribs from the waves, stunt kites
clack even though it's dark, out through the slats of the bunk,
or mackerel flop on rocks, somehow drawn to the island.

Once, one body made an island, me – a skerry –
swaddled in mum. She cradled me over the rocks,
leaned my face to a cauldron of waves,
and later, in the bunk, arms pinioned me in the dark.

Here ensconced in sunlit dark, a storm besets the island.
I peer out from my knee-cramped bunk
as a wheelchaired old woman – is it mum? –
heals her breast with waves, throws her wig out over the rocks.

It's Penmon, going off those rocks, houses miniatures
in the dark, and the tide, slanting shark fin waves,
tugs me back to the island. Some impostor's there
in place of mum. The ladder's fallen from the bunk.

In the darkness, these brain waves pulse in my bunk,
the mattress an island where I rock...
Get out of my head, you're nothing like mum.

POSTCARD FROM CEMAES BAY

A postcard I await, delayed, waylaid as they are
with worries, insurance concerns.
I see a harbour of shingle stars, statics on the headland.
Gulls, overheard.
Fingers, arthritic, hold a Samsung,
signal inconsistent, bars and charge.
His brain blown, years ago, a faulty radio,
burnt circuits. He knows his valves, his ohms.

When the card arrives, she won't sign stepmother
or surrogate aunt.
No solace with her nursing past.
She's all thumbs and aphasia, as the sea crackles,
drowns her voice.
Her heart I touch through its skeletal cage.
His heart shut, no knowledge to impart,
no assurance from afar, stuck as they are.

A promenade of invalids, ice creams;
cliques of outpatients, hip replacements,
stains on their nation, absorb tabloids,
dosette boxes, visit news agents.
The conspicuous absence of babies, lives of colour;
whispers of 'picaninnies', 'queers',
against a backdrop of gannets,
guillemots, and, more faint, the fulmar.

The sea's atmosphere highlights the white
of rollers. Porpoises nose to the surface.
Terns land, outmoded aircraft.
I picture a wind farm, hear its hum; arms wave –

a shipwrecked survivor.
Oystercatchers dive, Wylfa's waste on sand.
And no card arrives. Its edges hold disaster,
like disaster holds the bad star.

In the absence of post, shades of bees hit caravans.
Awnings flap, the guise of ghosts.
Sky seals their asylum, end of life plans.
It's a sort of anteroom, awaiting the sea's encroachment,
while curlews and whimbrel retreat to fields,
linger like thumbprints.
Beach huts crawl with lice and love,
pastel coloured, house shells and skulls.

Through father's eyes, too dim to pick a postcard,
on a picnic chair, Llanbadrig in shadow,
a toy chapel, spire a stalk to sunlight.
A gauge tramway's varicose vein.
My seascape a pier, a spine, vertebrae fused.
This is where the end begins: legacies,
new wet dreams; phantom scents, salted herring,
the bob of boats moored unattended.

SPIDER

To the lintel — and there just a *thing*,
trembling hosiery. Fishnet thick

that black snarl against stucco,
that pinwheel galaxy, mons pubis —
silk steadying over a fan heater.

October's false widows prise their way
in. No Wi-Fi, nothing to contain
the vacant web with names
like *orb-weaver, Araneidae, house, garden...*

And so I resort to something worse —
the glove of a werewolf suit,
green stars off the tops of tomatoes
or simply a shadow of legs on the ceiling.

Since in the middle of that mass of neither
vegetable nor mineral — up by the lintel —
a white hole portends nothing

but a sudden quickening.

SURVIVAL HORROR

Having got past the loft with its lunging beast,
rummaged through the piano,
my avatar consigned afternoons to Derceto Manor.
A dark mirror of school:
dragged by a zombie to the tune of Chopin's *l'Adieu*.

With each resurrection I was more skilful
with my fists, shotgun or sabre,
vigilant too in saving prior to exploring new rooms.
Each night I filed myself at the foot of a staircase,
moving through catacombs.

I slept on problems, no web access or walkthroughs,
let my psyche be the house,
my dream be the labyrinth, my self be the haunting.
A polygon and inventory,
lumbered with a biscuit box, oil lamp, statuette,

retreading footsteps, dealing with angry paintings,
Indian arrows, axe-throwers, I died
many times over. I leafed through occult books
for clues on how to kill winged sentinels on the balcony.
The grimoire on a giant worm:

its words were instant death.
Evading library vagabonds, the hardest part,
duelling with the pirate or blasting carnivorous birds.
I was most scared by the laugh of Pregzt.
Who am I? – I'd ask myself.

A gramophone played *Danse Macabre* to ghosts of dancers.
The key was on the chimneypiece.
Bullies in the cupboard, under the trapdoor, the chest.
I failed to trigger a secret mechanism.
Saved on a disk in the loft: this stasis of adolescence.

LIGHTHOUSE

Here stands my body, a sea-washed tower,
its pose anorexic, clothed on a catwalk.
My stance fixed, chic self-centredness,
while out of sight, monasteries of Puffin Isle.

My eye a thousand candelas, mass of fireflies.
The sky, a mirror, mirrors decades of lightning.
No keeper in my brain-case, a bell unclanging.
And if that bell's a tongue, my song's

stuck with rust. Inside my hooped heart
somewhere, a transistor wireless, unplugged,
having recorded last a shipping forecast.
By night, rocks watch over me like ghouls.

The shore's a bore, ants of saloons and canoes
carry the same summer, always the same
silhouetted look. Always summer. Where are they
in winter storms? Where are they when rain

lashes my glass? Gargantuan, grey on grey,
waves whip a shawl around me. Where are
they in this Nordic noir? Waves hang on photos,
stilled explosions. Half inside a cloud,

stucco houses, cereal boxes turned inside
out. The lifeboat station, abandoned, could be
Venice, could be the Seine, if I squint slightly.
Only motor boats harass me on hot Julys.

What of the sun? The sun's a smudge the best
of times. The sun's a gun that hasn't been fired.
Again, in summer, I see myself a child, myself
clambering rock pools, femurs not fully grown.

He fires crackers, a cap gun. His father throws
out a fishing line, a leaded weight. His father
faces sideways, turns away. By night, gas light
of schooners, some distant, nautical mile.

By night, sirens comb their hair on the cliffs.
By night, his father, the very father, him.

FROM THE UPSTAIRS WINDOW

Mother doesn't know me now. Hours beat like a metronome.
Sunrise strobes ever-faster on the sofa. Rain veins down
the window. It beads for hours in the downpour.

Bachelor curtains smack of the same yellow serving hatch.
Ghost decor. Must have fetched it from a photo. Even my rug
is retro. Carpenters chords on the radio. Mother sung
by the cassette recorder. Fondue pots boxed or let go.

Over the road, years line up bungalows of what I've become.
Decades ago she wanted to try for a girl – South Drive or
High Meadows? – who knows now the hours slide indoors

past yucca where flows a familiar five o'clock smell of soup
readied and served in new households. All seems as it was:
uneventful – and still I'm drawn to woodsmoke, barracks,
winters when snow was four feet high. Where did it go?

Even though they've long since papered walls, even though
Betamax and *Star Wars* toys are pushed to the attic, dreams
never let go, never move on. I'm left staring at floorboards.

Mother calls in repeats of spring, links daffodils to melanoma.
Dreams slander her voice...

Father sleepwalks. Sun-kissed dementia on cruise ships
with his new partner. Water-damaged film goes unrestored...

Regrets pile on the sofa – the art college girl with angel wings
I was too shy to talk to, the lesbian, the one with the cello
who got back with her ex, the one who preferred her lecturer...

And when hours weigh their shades on sills, it's the end of summer.
Not school this time, rather a nursing home. To forget it all
except the wrench from mother's arms. This is the place it starts.
To forget the names I strove so hard to grasp.

INSOMNIAC

When sleeplessness comes
I take myself to Pluto. Out of body I soar
to that ice planet surface. To escape the day,
dumb circuits of thought, I go to Charon's limb –
curtains drawn, lights off, an intrepid astronaut.
To switch myself off, I warp
to Nix, Styx, Kerberos the dog. Or I teleport,
pineal eye, out of the bedroom –
superluminal, shun the moon, reach solitude.

I slip to an underworld, remote. I survey
the tundra, stalagmites, hexagons
of ice, mirror-like planes, a vast plateau.
Above me, a star field on Cthulhu Regio
('the whale'), dragon scales, the dark side
of a dwarf. Weightless, almost. I've landed
though lost, visor fogged. Under lids, I wish
for airlessness, to freeze instantaneous,
crack like a rose frozen in a Petri dish.

Behind me, no spaceship. I suffer the cortisol,
thoughts of *her*, not waking up...
Down the duvet, my legs sculpt a landscape,
fold chasms and peaks. Exposed, reds, pinks,
tholins, face a heart-shape. I turn and turn
like the six-hour day, going over nodes –
mother, father, lover, those spurned
or now silent. No escaping my orbit,
my barycentre of regret, gyring round this hub –

and this is death, this is death: the mind whirs on.

THE OTHER SIDE

Sun-dogs over the bay, this haze a portal
to where I left a skin behind:
under cliffs where a windbreak stood –

catching barbecues, a waft of hot dog fat –
kids, open mouths, white noise, torn kites,
tugging pants for treats, tugging nan's;

dads tugging hands of ozone-scorched pink.
Cirrus streaks cream-on-blue from gadabouts,
faces singed around sunblock and shades.

A photo of the bay: ghosts through acetate –
all bathed in August – roving
this inlet; or waxworks waving to waves,

to boys, like buoys bob towards the sound,
drowned out by a jet, far out.
A cloud rack covering us, brother and I

toeing the sea-bed for hazards – waist-high,
half-mile, wading down a sand-slope,
in-jokes of slipping off the sea's shelf.

In lucid dream, surf starts again to move,
the beached mannequins resume,
re-stage that day; light remains just as lurid –

like I've landed, an intrepid time-traveller.
To where? Mother, her eighties-dark hair –
impossible – revived, ashore, a wraith

of her, ensconced in a diorama.
If only I could clamber through this gloss,
fit through this frame, to where is forbidden.

BOXES

The day of your funeral,
more tender than usual,
I'd forgotten what tears
were: even at your grave
they couldn't break through.
Numbness ensued on
its subsidence: your box
under tonnes of earth.

Now a box of *things*: your
priest-given rosary ring,
a clock stopped, the precise
time its batteries ran out;
tear-stained notes from
your bedside; a wristband;
a hand-written epigraph
in my Klee monograph...

A certain weight in the
ether, or rained-in, loose-
end occasion, takes us
back, opening up. All this
obeys its reason, exists
as crypts, unprocessed
feeling. Boxes, unsealed,
need to be sealed again.

Some of us have boxes,
and, in those, *more* boxes,
some of which are without
a key. Even shrinks can't
find a way in. Some are
closed as a corpse in a
sunless, silk-lined room.
So what slips through?

Moments of promises:
a box of scrolls that some-
times unroll. Can't be sure
of the trigger, the cause,
as the clasp unlocks. I
sense the build-up. *Rush* –
the timelessness of your
breath escapes the room.

DREAMS OF DECEASED LOVED ONES

They float like cells inside the eye,
interlope, drift over throws, each morning,
melt on the chaise longue. Dreams, sure invaders,
appear in sepia, film held up to light.
A ghost zone of fury, phantasmagoria,
unblinking darkness, this slideshow
occurs on springs of a mattress.
They come diaphanous, extra colourful,
butterflies, the uninvited, through windows,
pointlessly so. *Where?* – like asking
where the starlings go, where autumn leaves go.
Seeming messages, envelopes I cannot open.
Then shafts of sun lift feathery thoughts,
or souls lighter than my handkerchief.

REVIEW OF THE TITANIC MUSEUM

All is negative space, perched on the stern, face out to Belfast harbour.
Everything to scale. The slipway's rib cage with stanchions of a gantry
that once gave flesh to this. I pace the keel, a ghost. White lines imply
dimensions. I imagine soap in the runnels, imagine tonnes of soap, oil
for the gigantic hull to slide, a public cry and celebrate with streamers.
Nothing in the dockyard. Just the odd seabird, shadow on the plaza.
A lonely funnel, like a de Chirico. No souvenir, though I ask myself
what I'd give for a rivet? What *would* I give for a rivet? All I find is a
shell tossed by the tide. I make my way along and back to the tour
guide, to the group on segways in expensive suits. I dig the architecture,
how the facade is the same height as the bow and the same shape; how
its windows glitter like fish scales. Behind me they're dancing on graves
in replica clothes, staged photos. I wonder if Auschwitz is like this.
I wonder if Auschwitz is full of merchandise and Disney rides and
babyccinos. I wonder what kind of toll there is. I prefer air outside.
I prefer this cast-iron sunlight. I prefer my dark tourism of strolling
this length, this width, imagining myself on deck, the promenade by
lifeboats, knowing something everyone else didn't. The sombreness
of cabinets in old fashioned museums: I prefer the childlessness, the
inwardness, unsmiling interiors.

WHAT HAPPENED TO NAN?

1)
When sleep comes the cortège stops by cairns,
tugs the silver cord, nearly always with ravens.

Only here, snapped back to white chairs, dew,
do I recover details – umbrella faces,

black suits, cousins, hatchbacks, clunk shut.
A day off school, same uniform, blazer apt.

Puce curtains close. Organ music. Brother's hand
round my elbow. His only touch, never since.

Curtains shut, hymn books, mahogany pews,
priest's robe. I knew nothing of the electric trolley,

nothing of the antechamber, ID tag, oven,
adjustment of gas, spray to prevent flashbacks;

nothing of the raking of ash, how it's
the thigh-bone, the skull, that remain as cakes.

Uncle cowed by the casket, looking once, not long;
there scorched, already, the after-image.

2)
Waking – on the wall, the hospice, curious
how they got her ring off, who that was, the ring

that dug its way in, what marriage meant. She said
they'd have to amputate, was the only way.

Who kept the book of condolence, sent light
to career through catkins, starring the eiderdown?

Her thoughts mended, there to remember us
by. She must hold this smile, her favourite

child of three. Or might she actually forget?
As she went of course through walls, up and out.

I asked such naive questions, and was shown
a red admiral moored on a Volvo. 'She's there

returned.' So soon, I thought. And what of us,
that limitless repertoire of love, was it stored

under antennae?, or was it circling somewhere
close?, or, unsaid till now, lost with her warmth.

REVENANT

Sometimes *#9 Dream*, the bay window radio,
amid airwaves, lyrics, or cafes through the day.
They carry you through the membrane.
More vivid on anniversaries, as the sick light of May
sinks like a knife through epidermis.
And a sense of close-knit consciousness,
unable to write replies on letters overnight,
letters for you to sign. As if you know
I couldn't stomach a full apparition,
you manifest where the mind can handle.
Though is it kinder I wonder, any less tense,
when you turn the house back into a gurney,
the bed where you slept into a hoist?
I don't see the purpose, what good it does.
It's not as if those words are heard
as you lip them like bubbles undersea.
Worse, hoodwinked back to that hospital stench,
pleading again for pills to doctors,
priests, impostors, miracle workers;
witness wooden crosses, hair falling out...
And what is it with the zombie towns we visit? —
always travelling to faraway cities, trains
without stations, cars without drivers...
Why do elders stagger about like imbeciles?
And why're grandpa and grandma strangely living?
What's the point of wails, white noise, garbled tannoys?
Maybe kinder — no more comprehensible —
than blow light bulbs on your birthday,
sure this is the place to convene, under the blanket
of my eyelids, safe among the arachnids.

THE BUNGALOW

It started with the word *glaucoma*, a tunnel,
a card game, a question on the queen of diamonds
and the jack of hearts.
    It ended with a smudge of grey through glass,
and mother winding her way down your path,
the uncut grass, her legs through the fence;

a bouquet, freesias I think, handed back.
Me in the car, I wasn't meant to see you. You,
your hair white, frizzed, albino-like. Like you,
partial sight, as mother's coat eclipsed you,
    in your bungalow, a crypt,
once home of karaoke, endless toast and jam.

I tried to convince you the queen of diamonds
could be confused for the jack of hearts. I lied;
and in your eyes I saw you see right through me,
white lies beyond my years.
    Forsaken by Christ, your box of psalms
were no longer read; they festered in your dresser.

I too, in time, left you in your rocking chair,
the vestibule. By your side a wireless, dead-eyed,
distant, limbs thin, slumped with static and fuzz.
    Only in dreams came the transmissions:
your brain, demented through lead in your pipes,
the hum of pylons above.

Then the amnesia-white of your walls, the traces
in those spaces you'd vacated. All false teeth
and playing cards, divvied up by uncles and aunts,

and by mother too. She kept a box of morbid
souvenirs.

She talked of grandpa, only later, dragging
you from room to room.

GHOST STORY

It arrives in strips   torn out of a compendium of dreams. It begins as wisteria up the walls   a boarded-up window   a gable   another window   dark as an eye-patch. It's something I've meant to write for some time. Each night another vignette is unveiled   as if viewing a mural by torchlight. It's always a darkness beyond darkness   like once in the attic with a shade no photons could escape or where such darkness festers   in oubliettes   undercrofts   outside with rooks and a sense of the venerable. Often it's a house I've once been in   one with a tumble-down facade   sheer cliffs on every side. Last night   the house of a married couple or mausoleum   its door-turned-tombstone carved in exotic ciphers. I chucked a grappling hook over the roof to the other side   hoisted myself through a spider-filled frame. All I remember was a presence of husband and wife   how I kept opening doors to bedrooms or staircases   or doubling back on myself   finding rooms were running out   or floral walls closing in. Shut in the vestibule   I sought the bustle of the streets. Shrieks out of a letterbox met with nothing but disinterest.

UNE VILLE ABANDONÈE

A pedestal shorn of its statue, the sea's encroachment,
eye socket windows, absentees. Wind, on the *banlieue*.
The reek of medieval atmosphere. Belfries, the unringing
of bells, the town square, the broken parapet, the tumbleweed
street. Here, all shadows in the sun, here the last man. Ask
where the people have gone; ask and the answers trail off
on the breeze. The sky lowers whiteness, a morgue sheet.
Cobblestones hold the clatter of clogs: stored recordings.
Doors, no doorknobs or latches. Shutters are shut blind
and all is static.

        This, my future ennui. A shrine, relics,
where the town's your shroud, wraps itself round your
recluse heart, occult pulse, your spectral hood. Alone
on a bridge, you're a beguine or anchorite, then Ophelia:
your face ashen, hair camouflaged, sprawling. I see myself
sketch your vignette, as gables double themselves over quays.
This grief has yet to happen: a lock of hair in my pocket,
the sea rising up the church spire. The sleep of poppies
drifts through me, with you in exile, a deposed queen.

WHAT YOU CALL YOUR 'WINTER MODE'

On the wicker chair I wait for the duvet's rise:
you're just a mound, breath,
as I worry over why, again, you've overslept.
Could it be early effects of menopause?
    Mid afternoon again,
Sunday shrieks of five-a-side across the park;
your shade's rise and fall, minus it seems the astral part;
through the newsfeed tingle on your phone,
morning show, radio (one that never sleeps),
my stifled pant from up the grove...
    No alarm, just Diazepam,
as you turn to expose the mole under your eye,
'tear of a Pierrot', 'wrist scars' of which you joke.

Do I laugh? *No* –
    you've made a sickroom for us both,
made a sickroom of us both
(or what you call your 'winter mode');
made the day's camera roll, unsaved to Skydrive or Cloud...
    as I think of the base of your back, sacroiliac,
your broken ballet dancer toe, your 'womb pain';
I think of your blood, your bowel, your mother
'like this her age', juggling Naproxen and Co-codamol.
I think of your liver, think of your organs, think
still of your brain in its skull as you sleep;
I think of your sunken eye sockets,
the flight of your face in dream.

AMONG THE MOONFISH

Jellies, moons, man-o-war, polkadot the sand's carpet.
Stranded by sea, jellies line the beach,
a sort of purgatory, part night terror.

Moons recur, among fish and spindrift:
pack-a-mac, umbrella, poking a squid till it shoots
its ink, a dark cloud; tip on each bell, a purple heart.

This, the start of feeling afraid: saucers
like sci-fi, or footage of piled genocide.
Organs too are like this, water-filled, strange.

A wash of polyps, the sea spreads them evenly.
Crystalline, trees electrified by lightning
reanimate, nightly, as the tide moves invisibly.

Omens, moments like these: the sun needles
through cloud, takes a biopsy; a glitter of razor shells
readying themselves for theatre.

Surgeons are seabirds: they scan, clear the carnage,
go about their business, before stingers
unfurl, return, like shadows on an X-ray.

ECHOES

in nuclear medicine, corridors like infinity mirrors.
Everything screams off silver surfaces, lift doors,
gurneys, forks in the refectory... I'm there early.

Before visiting hours, smokers in slippers mingle
by ambulances. I follow echoes, lurch past nurses.
In triage, invalids clasp eye patches, vomit in papier-mâché.

Echoes of doors slamming, a clatter of crutches;
the chaplain's picture in the prayer room (he gave
her funeral), an omen of the same shit recurring

(sunlight on her face, I tried to make it permanent;
tears on her arm, watching them flow like rivers;
pushing the emergency alarm, no one running).

I lie awake, refuse faith since the ground gave way,
a trapdoor to a place beyond all hope, metaphysics.
Consultants, not consultants, *assassins*; the chaplain,

not a chaplain, *the Reaper*; things, things, full of layers.
Upstairs, a scan rules out a cyst, anything benign.
My mind's haywire, a glitterball. Each facet, valid;

they splinter, curse, a kaleidoscope of happenings.
Two time zones, concertinaed, a kind of shell shock
(mother in her wheelchair, biliousness, daffodils).

Synapses fire. The amygdala, out of sync, thinks
I'm war torn, a sniper's crosshairs on my temple;
or better, Russian roulette in my head. The cylinder rolls...

I fear electrodes, matchsticks under my lids.
I vent my rage on inanimate things, lash out,
brake my hand on a bin, livid at the stars, providence.

It doesn't exist, though even now a vestige of belief.
Upstairs a syringe finds the surest vein. She sleeps,
hangs on. A monitor bleeps. My love,

I swallow a valium; and the heartbeat slows, my breathing slows,

sweat dissolves, the dizziness, shaking slows. No more echoes

(the chair's just a chair to sit upon, the nurses

are just healers, the chaplain, just a chaplain,

and daffodils, in the communal garden, just flowers

which bow and waver).

A FORESHADOWING

Looked for, the abandoned lido –
just ghosts of swimmers,
bikini-clad sunbathers – shoulders singeing.
Our day of dark tourism:
wading through the coolness of dunes
towards ruins of outhouses.
Our summer of surgery,
escape to the beach, combing a trove of artefacts.
Pine trees angular through the seasons;
gorse waved hands from chalet windows.

Losing ovaries, we craved shapes
not holes in things. You scraped ovals
in the sand – 'every oval a face' –
and screened the omens out.
A patch of oyster shells: smithereens stumbled on.
An ossuary? For you, an Elysian Field,
the cemetery of a shoal, your phantom womb.
The rictus by your navel,
'just another scar', stitches, misaligned stars;
stars you'd string into constellations.

On dune slack we moved to Nicotine Path.
Through shaded eyes our shadows
stretched towards strandline garbage.
Gazing back – stripped turkeys,
a blockade of bodies, the heat's haze –
from the pastiness of our faces.
The tea man with coke tin lanterns talked relapse
as we sipped on plastic chairs.
Silence. We skipped over cracks, single file,
past the burnt-out hotel's blackened windows.

THE THING

Waking fully, what it was was a thing,
a black tentacled thing, coming at me, smothering me.
Its eyes pooled into me, spider-like, legion.
It moved through a metamorphosis:
fog to the blackest octopus. I fought it off –

wrestled, sparred with it, used aikido techniques;
still the thing charged, inky incubus,
untangling itself on the sheets.
It came again and I fought it. I thumped it,
punched it, threw it across the room

where it landed on the clothes-maid.
It wriggled there for a moment like some eels,
tentacles dangling.
Again it came, kamikaze, flying at me,
arms spread, star-shaped.

Its breath the whiff of a fly infested seal,
its face a crab's back happy accident.
Appendages wormed around my wrists.
It wanted, I think, to be swallowed, sink down
my esophagus, multiply in my nourishing insides.

I pushed off its mandibles.
It wanted my lips, my tongue, to be complete;
a zygote in every cell, insidiously, unbeating, reaching
like a rhizome under flesh.
I gave an almighty heave, let out a scream,

bashed it against the wall.
Some gunk spewed out an orifice.
It must have caught sight of itself in the window glass.
Only a candle to glint its shine and filth.
It saw itself: just a thing, as nothing, monstrous.

It vomited upon seeing itself –
then *puff*, plumed back into amorphousness.
'For now,' I said, 'I've won.'
The room listened, played mute witness.
Inside the body's catacombs it sleeps like an angel.

THE WAITING ROOM

Upstairs, she starts her chemo; down here it's limbo.
Down here, an anteroom where outpatients mingle.
   Everything tinged with the unreal:
from plasma screens to the walls and the vending machine –
its crisps and sweets glint with surplus significance.
   The nurse offers me water melon, hands me Allsorts;
the nurse smiles like no angel, a smile unreadable.

Upstairs, a cannula's attached to her arm. Assistants whisper
and carboplatin gets pumped through the heart's blood
to zap the cells gone astray since surgery.
   Here that's about all I know, with uncertainty.
No one talks, not even couples beside each other
in the bucket chairs.
Though the ghosts in the empty ones talk. They talk to me.

Sometimes pates like kiwifruit appear. To them it's routine.
Or at least it's the face worn through the revolving door.
   No signs, no nothing besides the hints of seriousness.
They just sit, spouse to spouse, taking seats in a cinema.
   Blood's taken, again and again, like there's no price on it,
there's no tomorrow.
Upstairs again her blood's taken, somewhere up the elevator.

Down here's a saint. She lathers the floor with disinfectant,
glories at the weather, bleach her Bible.
   My headscarf makes me look like a patient. But I have respite
and magazine racks for distraction. I have, I think, repression.
   Names called for judgment – Anthony, Margaret, Denise –
then they disappear.
Upstairs they go, living out their stories.

And up there I picture those still staggered at their passing:

Celia, reading her newspaper,
and mother, folding her gown —

doing usual chores on the top floor, currently out of bounds.

WINTER PICNIC

We sit by a tearoom. Scooters, hula hoops, scuttle and clack.
We deserve a rainbow – though what do I know?

We're taking notes, each wanting a winter poem.
Dylan on the veranda, the radio inside, we smile

and tap iPhones. We visit lovebirds in our minds,
the aviary closed. I photograph doves, mid-flight,

for a video which later you'll compose.
I twist the top off a gingham jar, after you loosen it;

our flask a third term between us. We lock hands,
the lamps switch on, stoop over avenues. We twine

fingers, staring at the sky together. The sky
is one immense snow globe, and the sleet beads

on the fence, lachrymose. Trees mesh like happy skeletons.
You talk of soundtracks, recording your love:

woodpigeons, dogs, distant chirrups. No ganache,
you spoon chocolate cake, offer me yours. We handfast –

while the winter goes on, goes on, while sea sounds
of the motorway lead to reverie. I want days

like this, going on, days of no real schedule,
watching birds pick at crumbs – *with* you, not beyond...

It's February. We sit here, sharing illness, kissing,

drawing faces round knots. We watch as dusk falls

on ruins of the park's mansion. We listen, while air pincers
through the ginkgo biloba. God, let us go on.

I want us to hold here till the sun burns out.
I move because my legs are numb, just that, I want you to know.

LOVE SONG ON LONGWAVE

Boxed here, her room, fruit punch served as breakfast,
no TV, bad reception, books on architecture,
more on trees, runes, in dust.
The mattress, as ever, unshaped to my skin, bones;
and so the pain goes, comes in waves.

Now the radio, its waves, long and lonely,
and she and I in every note.

Each point, the scan finds some instrument,
some aria, far flung, from the far reaches of time zones.
She and I in every note, transatlantic, beyond the static,
under shadows of satellites, transitions of planets,
across oceans of waves, long and short.

Nothing but French rap, faint jazz, something cool,
not in my language.

Violins take us to Prague, cellos to Munich, the harp
takes us out of body, beyond the clouds –
like signals depart – a slow sail to outer bounds,
out to the stars, where, my love, *we* reside. I hear us
back between stations, frequencies, mistuning
the dial, delirious.

For now, another room, through drywall,
in whatever waves may soundproof her sleep.
It's quiet now, but for the chainsaws of morning,
the wireless off at the wall.

So how can I *know*, somewhere our love is playing,
out of a smartphone, bluetooth earphone, she and I
in every note, beyond this room, in waves long and short.

Cats scratch occasionally, run their arms round
the door's gap, like tarantulas.

And as I gather my clothes, escape the chainsaw,
sour fruit punch, windowsill and drought of company,
September's shadows lean from poplar trunks.

MORNINGS

Spires of heathens, through the pane, through a slit of voile.
Dawn aches higher, its chorus inspiring the bedridden.
A wood pigeon, pinned to last scraps of dark. The sky's hue,
greyish-purplish-blue. Shadows on telegraph wires.

I peer down. Cars pull out. Mothers in suits, business class.
School kids bruised, led by wrists: machine-moulded citizens.

Without you, I lose myself in the damask of the sheets,
down a valium, slip into dream,
where cheek-to-cheek selfies stay intact.
Bank holiday sirens, fading out.

I want days to never begin, for stars to rise, drift again –
to a trashed cityscape, towerblocks in tatters, papers strewn,
the scene post-nuclear, streets crazed with driverless cars.
To wake is to jump off a high rise.

MARTYRS TO EACH OTHER

Now the treatments have passed

I see the shape of Wales in the clouds. You tell me to 'go there,
anywhere but here.' *Just days now*, where we, a pair condemned,

gaze different ways. Now the treatments have passed, your fingers
fidgeting craft won't say how you feel. Your thoughts, a country

I cannot reach. The one outside the ward, easier to see. Should
I find a nimbus in your bruise, should I? Now the treatments

have passed, those stars are the work of cannulas. Your shoulder
blades, riddled with roadmaps, full of furrows I anoint, final acts

of love. I caress your swollen legs, your bed sores. Now the
treatments have passed, I massage your sacroiliac, place packs

at the base of your back, say goodbye to your breasts, goodbye
to your legs, goodbye *mons pubis*. My kiss lives on your forehead.

Now the treatments have passed, drinks I fetch from the fridge
are a pittance. My hands are healing hands. Surely you need no

oxygen mask. Now the treatments have passed, your hair unsheds –
an evergreen? All pristine aside from cells which surge

like an army, your ballooned kidney attached to a tube,
attached to bags. Now the treatments have passed, I'll

be your Christ when you lend me your balm. Or am I your Magi
as I bring you gold (a ring worn to X-ray), frankincense (a final

attempt), myrrh shipped from eBay? My gift: to hold this grief
for you, take home the debris of visits which clutter the room.

My love, you'll be my Christ. I'll wear the scar.

THE BITTER END

No, this will never beat us,
when she's moaning, rocking for morphine.
I say to *you* – who's insidious,
hides cowardly along the linings of organs –
that love will win, love will grow stronger
with each howl it puts her through.
Love will win, it *must* – and if sickness
assumed a form we'd beat you to a pulp.
A slanting wind starts in our side room,
ceiling tiles gently lifting
as though there's a spy above us.
The wind, like arms around the room,
moves over her bruise, threads through the wiring.
I take my chance to say *everything*.
The wind roars through summer windows.
She sleeps. Painlessness is all that matters;
my creaking voice recedes through shutters.
Nurses add a dose for the driver.
                                    For her it's respite –
though I wanted her to hear my tears.
No concealment between lovers.
Her kidney drains amber like sun on the sky's spires.
I hold back from stroking her bangs.
I see her socks twitch in search of the sheet's touch.
Her abdomen, stitched like a doll, is a battle of zig-zags.
I dare you to show yourself – *sadist*, *bastard*...
Are you the one who taunts through the window slats?
I watch her nose-tube steal milk from her stomach.
I catch her angel-face, safe on my pillow.
This must be what it means to die well.
The air is clearer, and my tears

have dried on my face like cellophane.
Shamelessly I wear them, my only protest.
When she sleeps I write – and here, and here is revenge.

ELSEWHERE

13.6.17
The ambulance wends its way through conifers. All screams
déjà vu. They give you room 16. It reminds me of our hotel
in negative. I share a sense of prescience. You on a gurney
say 'it's by design' – which again was expected...
    Shuffled in, a glass door opens to a garden of squirrels.
Close, the jingle of an ice cream van. You slurp a cornetto,
sure it'll make you puke. A final wish, with fizzy lemonade.
Ice cubes too on tap. Ice gold, nil by mouth. Every sip bliss.

14.6.17
Doctors crowd around with clipboards, a welcoming party –
prophets of doom, smiling receptionists. We list objectives.
They come, go; they begin sentences with *So*. You ask to be
'safe, happy.' I talk of 'art class, garden visits, lucid chats...'
    Outside, benches where we'll slow & squeeze a lifetime,
pretend our future veranda. This jolts a small resurrection –
'fling open the doors, windows,' you cry, 'let the squirrels in.'
I comply. Wind catches a curtain, sends the cactus spinning.

15.6.17
By day more dreamlike than dream, a way-station. The light
is tinged, a Polaroid – like this already happened, was meant.
The full sunlight, inappropriate, the solstice ill-timed, spent,
as I sit by your bedside, whisper though light-headedness...
    I say everything again – everything I want to say. Words
dense, right into your ever-waking ear. The final sense. Last
words. You requesting your hair washed, the hairdresser &
aroma lady. So random. Far from drama. Such non-events.

16.6.17

Then a comatose day. Corridors, nodding nurses, nulled time,
snack bars, numbed out, peering through slats, wax, soap-like,
Madame Tussauds, open mouths. No yawn. By night to your
door, moth-like, your lamplight through the nightmarish gap.

I catch your breath, nothing else. Nonetheless, it's etched,
taken back to the camper bed. Routinely I enter, reassure you,
how close my vigil. Quick before leaving I kiss your forehead.
By dawn I'm told your lips are white. I check your fingertips.

17.6.17

Outside's sickly warm again. Volunteers knee-deep in weeds,
lawnmowers dragging a din. Likewise, inside, hoovers mutter,
say we're earthly still. Vitals no longer matter — just measures
of distress. The room smells of cabbage. Your skin porcelain,

hair spread, Pre-Raphaelite. A CD spins, those loathsome
notes, panpipes. You talk with one eyebrow. That & twitches
of your cruicked arm. Your lips paralysed. A straw no longer
knocks a nose pipe. Your hands warm, as they were at home.

18.6.17

I dim your side lamp with a scarf. The Gestapo bulb overhead
gives me a migraine. Syringe drivers bleep (end a programme),
& the sparrows sing like it's a normal day. Pine trees surround
the grounds, while the observed breaths & beats are primitive.

Through doors, dandelion seeds swarm, souls in June heat.
They drift, orbs. They drift, fall. They are, I say, past residents.
A pastor offers a sticking plaster. I confess — ask to follow you
to fields of patchy grass, roundabouts. I dream of tumbleweed,

19.6.17
wait for a knock at my door, on pins, wait for a knock, news
of a change of rhythm. Hours pass, lighting candles, listening
to *News 24*. Panic managed, diazepam, a fact sheet. A scream,
withheld, says why are you not doing more? Surely a remedy,
        a vestige of belief. I just mop your legs with frankincense.
All I do is say – again – how I'd gift you my every limb. This
as fatigue overwhelms. Cells go haywire, your body turns on
itself. A bee stinging. Which stings & takes the consequence.

20.6.17
Vinyl butterflies cling to your bed & you'll never notice them.
They take the place of eloquence. I recycle those same words,
repeat them again. I kiss your fringe, stroke your lobe, mourn
those wispy bits on your cheekbone, lashes the nurses praise...
        I call to angels in agnostic space. I'm here for the vapours,
for the portents. I'm here as witness. Only now should I pray?
Enough of this horror show. Enough of this pincushion flesh.
Enough of vomit, faecal taste. *Enough's enough*, she finally says.

THE END

With the close of a hospice door, clunk of a saloon, tyres
on gravel: an ending if ever there was one. Let us slalom
round statues of Mary, grottos in grounds, funerary fetishes.

Let it end with handed-over possessions, towels, slippers,
photo off the wall (she never saw), smell of softened linens,
folded neatly with inventory, for no-one especially.

Ask for no heroes, villains, nick-of-time pliers on wires,
no H-bomb to defuse on the horizon. Ask for nothing
as the sun pops, extinguishes. Let it end as a balloon.

Let the chauffeur pull unsmilingly through the driveway.
Let the leaves fall sometimeish in September.
Let unhappy accidents happen on dual carriageways.

See father as a mannequin, us *both* as mannequins, feel
the numbness of thumbs on a gear lever, steering wheel
turn, sink in a blue lagoon, birds scatter from traffic islands.

Let doctors be anything but miracle workers. Sack Christ,
alienists. Insist the priest toddle off with his rosary beads,
chuck out his wooden crosses, fuck off to the hypermarket.

Pray only clouds on roads chaperone us. Stay on auto-pilot.
Read of St Bede's swiftness of sparrow down a dining hall.
Let's go art house, kino lounge a while.

Let bus stops hang unseasonal icicles, Belisha beacons
be lollipops if they want, the forget-me-nots freeze,
apocalyptic winter, denouement leave all threads a tangle.

Then *fin*, fade to dark. Stars drip to stalactites.

In the dream we kissed, kissing like we always did.
The evening after the microphones were set,
I said 'talk to me, please, talk however you wish.'

We shared that kiss, lips sewn up, eyes beyond
all language, your look of having witnessed.
I pursued you to this place, chased, trespassed,

your blindness cured, eyes to mine, first since
you pulled your hand away, frightened by love-hate.
I could see you'd seen me age. You said 'live',

did so through the weirdest mind link, privy
to my plan, shown to you – divine providence? –
as your lids twitched warm in the morgue. 'Go on',

in the midst of that kiss, where on our shore
a clam of time snapped shut, a bardo of sorts.
I asked to merge into us, tried for tongues,

the longest stay in your tarantula darkness.
Though just a room, still, for you a side room,
lucid, full of flowers, gizmos, dead-giveaways.

I wept buckets in front of your face, lips locked
still. We stood there. I couldn't breathe your air.
You said 'no, this is your limit, you cannot stay.'

SHADOWS ON THE CEILING

Hers was a dark Japanese aesthetic. She was in love with the lacquerware, the secret lives of silhouettes – morning, evening, night – and against our bright Gestapo bulbs. She loved the shadow play of fingers between our candles and ceiling, usually making cockatoos or butterflies dance and move and twine; her giving a voice to what she called our son et lumière. Sometimes, more by chance, the candelabra would cast a spider or chess piece – a knight or horse's head (and, like the nebula, we'd cherish it together). A puppet show would ensue around the rose plaster, while she mused on how erotic it was to show a little – an ankle or wrist – and how paleness is a virtue, how paleness *was* a virtue. I knew this to be beautiful. She juxtaposed our flesh, melanin, our limbs and skin tones almost identical. Beyond our bed, she made Shinto moves in the dark, praising the tiniest of trinkets, placing her faith in glints of moon in her eyes – serenading me with dreams of decoupage, bijou design, what she could do to lighten the dismal corners, adoring the web which appeared like a pylon. She'd glide through to the bathroom in a kimono, holding on to our sex – her sandalwood incense wafting in our perfect world; the kind of room she'd say where angels would descend to, push their noses in. That was then. Now, on my walls, the arching sun leaves tattoos (to remove them would leave a scar) and there's ghosting tints in crannies and nooks. The lamps she left are still lit, though they scream, and paper blisters and peels where once we laughed. The lintel, cornice and shades, they're changed; so too the mannequin heads, perfume, fishnets – feminine finery. I ask myself: what do I glean from these evening shadows – what does it mean to live in her place, loving such things, loving *her*, when it's just me and sedation? Votive charms, her hands once here, her art like a bruise which goes unseen, a moth flittering on this pillow beside me, my heart at one with the entropy.

NOTES AND ACKNOWLEDGEMENTS

The title *Full Sight of Her* makes reference to Sonnet XXIII by John Milton.

The word 'tain' in 'Black Mirror' refers to the tinfoil used in backing mirrors (from French, from *étain* tin, from Old French *estain,* from Latin *stagnum* alloy of silver and lead; see stannum).

Cover is *Light Document # 2* by Kim Parkinson. Original artwork appears in *The Grief Diaries*, Volume 4, Issue 4, 2019: http://www.thegriefdiaries.org/photography-by-kim-parkinson. *Interior and back cover photography by* Kim Parkinson. These form part of her *Light Documents* series, representing what she experienced through her blindness as a 'beautifully abstracted and tonally biased world.'

Final interior portrait of Kim taken by Patrick Wright. I wish to thank Todd Swift for his ongoing support and believing in my work, along with the rest of the Eyewear team.

I want to thank the following poets, each of which have had an influence on the revision process: Vona Groarke, John McAuliffe, Frances Leviston, and Gail Ashton.

My close friends were crucial in helping me to finish this collection: Rowan St Clair, thank you for the instress and affirmation of life; and Christine Burn, thank you for your prayers and understanding true love.

A special thank you to Bill Bodell for helping me through the process of grief.

Most of all though I want to thank Kim Parkinson, for the love, inspiration, art direction and feedback. I am forever indebted to your vision. Infinite kisses, my love.

Finally, I am grateful to the editors of the following publications in which some of these poems have appeared, sometimes in earlier forms. These are as follows:

The High Window, Ink, Sweat and Tears, Wasafiri, Agenda, The Reader, Poetry Space, London Grip, Plenitude, Degenerate Literature, London Magazine, Until the Stars Burn Out, Melancholy Hyperbole, Iota, Ricochet Review, Elsewhere, Caring Magazine, Ground Fresh Thursday, Allegro, Lunch Ticket, Poetry Quarterly, Brittle Star, The Ekphrastic Review, Ghostlight, Eunoia Review, DMQ Review, Envoi, The Blue Nib, The Manchester Anthology, Edify Fiction, and *The Poetry Village.*

'The End' was republished in *The Best New British and Irish Poets 2018* (Eyewear Publishing).